Advance Praise for *Your Blog, Your Business*

"Experts say that when business is slow, the last budget one should trim is advertising. *Your Blog, Your Business* lets a retailer have their promotions online and do it very nearly free." ~ Robert Ricciardi, President of About Face

"In thirty-five years in the industry, there are only a handful of retailers I have observed reach the success level of Carolyn Howard-Johnson. There is only one thing you need to learn from her to succeed . . . everything she says!" ~ Randy H. Eller, industry speaker, business consultant, and President Eller Enterprises, LLC

"As a columnist for *Home Décor Buyer*, Carolyn's no-nonsense approach to retailing and her easy-to-read writing style made her a coach to thousands of retailers." ~ Jim Carper, founding editor of *Home Décor Buyer*

"Carolyn's online marketing strategies make readers feel as if they are getting an inside tip from a good friend, not being sold on a product." ~ MaAnna Stephenson, Web site training and designs and author of Just the FAQs series of books on tech

Your Blog, Your Business:

A Retailer's Frugal Guide To Getting Customer Loyalty and Sales, Both In-Store and Online

By Carolyn Howard-Johnson

This Book Is Sponsored by
Gift Shop Magazine
(http://giftshopmag.com)

Published by HowToDoItFrugally Publishing
COPYRIGHT © 2010 by Carolyn Howard-Johnson

ISBN: 1451591047
EAN-13: 9781451591040
BISAC: BUS0570000 1. Business and Economics /Industries/ Retail 2. Marketing/ Retail/

Cover design by Chaz DeSimone Graphic Design (www.chazdesimone.com). Author photograph by Uriah Carr

Printed in the United States of America by CreateSpace.com.

Discounts are available for bulk quantity purchases of this book to be used for educational purposes, by social organizations, or for distribution by corporations or other business entities. Exclusive formatting and personalization is available for large-quantity orders. For more information, please contact HowToDoItFrugally Publishing at HoJoNews@aol.com.

Careers that are not fed die as readily as any living organism given no sustenance.

Dedicated to Patricia Norins, Editor of *Gift Shop* magazine, who generously sponsors this book and, looking ahead, the success of your blog.

"People get information in all kinds of ways now, and companies can no longer talk at the consumer. You have to engage in a discussion and let people create, discover, and share information and not just try to sell them things." ~ Howard Schultz, CEO Starbucks.

This slim book is part of the *Survive and Thrive* series for retailers. It is designed to help any independent retailer become *the* go-to store in town or online, and to do it frugally.

The cover of this book, designed by Chaz DeSimone (www.chazdesimone.com), uses Verdana and Georgia fonts, both designed by Mathew Carter for Microsoft, to be readable on computer screens even in small font sizes. They are often used as companions, Verdana as sans serif, Georgia as a complimentary serif choice. They are both commonly used by bloggers and Web site designers. The interior of this book is set in Times New Roman, a serif font traditionally used for books, newspapers . . . *and* blogs.

Your Blog, Your Business

Your adj. (possessive pronoun).1. Of or relating to you or yourself; belonging to you.

Blog n. 1.1998, short for weblog from (World Wide) Web + log. v. 2. The action of writing a blog.

Your adj. (possessive pronoun) 1. Of or relating to you or yourself; belonging to you.

Busí ness n. 1. Occupation, calling; also task, mission. 2. A commercial or industrial enterprise.

Your Blog, Your Business:

A Retailer's Frugal Guide To Getting Customer Loyalty and Sales, Both In-Store and Online

By Carolyn Howard-Johnson

This book is sponsored by
Gift Shop Magazine

HowToDoItFrugally Publishing
Los Angeles, California

Other Retail Books in the Survive and Thrive Series of Books for Retailers

A Retailer's Guide to Frugal In-Store Promotions: How To Increase Profits and Spit in the Eyes of Economic Downturns with Thrifty Events and Sales Techniques

Frugal and Focused Tweeting for Retailers: Tweaking Your Tweets and Other Tips for Integrating Your Social Media

Acknowledgements

Thank you to Patricia Norins, editor of *Gift Shop* magazine, for embracing the idea of sponsoring a book for the good of the community her magazine serves. Thank you to Debra Gold, president of Gold & Company and famous for buyer education programs she has produced from coast to coast. Because of her encouragement, this booklet and its *Survive and Thrive* cousins exist. Thank you to the folks at The National Stationery Show for encouraging me to launch the first HowToDoItFrugally book for retailers, *A Retailer's Guide to Frugal In-Store Promotions: How To Increase Profits and Spit in the Eyes of Economic Downturns with Thrifty Events and Sales Techniques*, and for continuing to support the series as part of their unique and stellar buyer education program. Thanks to author and former President of Gallery Décor and Carlan's and my life partner Lance G. Johnson for combing through early manuscripts for typos. Thanks for the talents of Chaz DeSimone who designed the cover, of John Quinn who inspired the retail series' upward arrow symbolizing better business ahead, and of Uriah Carr whose camera makes everyone look great. And thank you to many in the retailing and computer industries whose partnerships helped me hone the art of marketing with new media including blogs which have become my writing addiction.

Before We Get Started

My first *Survive and Thrive* book, *A Retailer's Guide to Frugal In-Store Promotions*, was designed to position any independent retailer as *the* go-to store for the products or services it sells. That book was based on my experience as founder and operator of independent gift shops serving several different clienteles. The second, *Frugal and Focused Tweeting for Retailers*, is based on my experience as a tweeter—from the beginning of Tweetdom—for retailers and my fellow authors. This book is a little down-and-dirty compilation of my experience with my own blogs and my experience contributing to uncountable others.

You'll notice I don't inundate you with lots of techy words. In most cases we can get by just fine with plain English. When I need some jargon—or think it important for you to know the terms—I've put them in bold typeface to cue you to turn to their definitions in the glossary of this booklet. It wouldn't hurt for readers new to blogging to peruse that section early on, especially if they are also new to much on the Web beyond e-mail.

Blogging is sometimes thought of as journaling—creative but far removed from the world of business. Don't you believe it! That doesn't mean that blogging for your business can't be creative and fun. Like a journal, it can (and possibly should) include anecdotes from your life, especially those related to your store.

I can't possibly cover all the possible places you might set up your blog. Rather, I give the simplest way to do it. If you are already an experienced blogger, you will still find much in this book for you. Practical suggestions of topics to blog about, as an example. Or ways to promote your blog so it will find readers and continue to attract more and more of them.

I want my books to be quick studies for retailers like you who want to focus on specific aspects of their marketing campaigns, in this case blogging and connecting that blog with your other online and in-store promotion. I hope this one boosts your entrepreneurial spirit and provides enough detail to take the fear (or dread!) out of doing what you must to carve your niche in the blogging world and attract those interested in stores, shopping, and the retail industry.

I also want to encourage brand-spanking new bloggers to go to Blogger (the service I recommend for easy blogging) as directed and take the first steps I describe to set up a blog. Do it as you read. My setup suggestions aren't fragile nor is the easy, schmeazy service I suggest. The basics of blogging are so simple you can hardly go wrong, but if you do (or just want to start over), your beginning efforts can be deleted.

A caveat here. I do *not* apologize for recommending resources I know and have used. I could take others' words for expertise, but firsthand knowledge is always better.

After a bit of playing and practice, I trust you will be so infatuated with the ease of the blogging process you'll move ahead with your new-found expertise. All to benefit your online marketing campaign . . . and, yes, your store.

Contents

1 ≋ The Basics: What Is Blogging, *Really*?

Writing is speech preserved. Speech as we think of it is what set humankind apart from all other life. Blogging is a casual way to use these gifts to benefit our businesses and ourselves.

Most of us who use blogs to promote think of them as something new, but they're not. Not really. "Chapbooks" were similar; they were used by itinerant vendors who wandered from village to village sharing their wares. Called "chapmen," these peddlars would leave in their customers' hands small booklets that they'd either give away or sell. That way, those who had come by their carts could share their offerings with others. The booklets were a kind of viral marketing (though it is certain the chapmen never heard the word "virus" or "viral"), an early marketing scheme that encouraged interaction between the sales person (or poet) and his customer, just as blogs do.

These little books were filled with drawings and descriptions of products, with the chapman's poetry or other literary efforts, or any mix of those elements. The chapman got to do what he pleased with his creative efforts, just as you do with your blog.

The basic concept of blogs is the same, but blogs let us reach farther and do our viral marketing faster than the chapman could.

And, of course, new technology requires new words. Human beings have always loved to put two words together to make new ones. So, now we have "blog"—a blend of the words "web" and "log" (and not a very good combination if you ask me). Nevertheless, it is an important concept for the marketing of products and services, and that's what we retailers do.

Blogs come in all different stripes, and—like the chapman—retailers can model their blogs to meet their own needs. They are described in current encyclopedias as regularly updated journals or newsletters that are easily accessible to the public because they are posted online. Those who write blogs report and comment on topics that interest them and their readers. They post their essays, notes, articles, or journal entries using software specifically designed to facilitate blogging called **content management systems** or **CMS**. They link to other Web sites in their blogs and may include photos, videos, and **podcasts** (mini audio or online radio segments). The most recent entry by the blogger is posted at the beginning of the blog, with earlier entries following in reverse chronological order. Visitors may respond to the blog after each entry and savvy bloggers encourage them to do so by asking questions, conducting polls, and participating in blog chains of like-minded bloggers who take a minute to add a note to their fellows' blog posts.

Blogs are ideally suited for retailers because they encourage one-on-one communication which builds loyalty and helps retailers know what their customers are thinking.

Your blog may consist of private information—or not. The blog pump should be primed with regular entries, but there are all kinds of ways to keep the workload to a minimum. (We'll discuss frugal use of your blog time later.) The important thing is that retailers learn to use a blog as a marketing tool that best fits their **branding** efforts. I'll talk briefly about branding before I lead you into six easy steps to starting a blog, so keep reading.

The other beautiful thing about blogs is that a writer needn't know a lot of techie stuff to use them. Gurus at blogging sites have already done the 100-pound lifting for those of us who are technically challenged. That is, these sites provide a choice of templates for your blog design, archives for your past posts, **labeling** (kind of like an index), and **search** functions (tech-talk for offering ways that the Internet world finds what you're doing with that blog of yours).

So here's to beautiful new relationships, relationships between you and your blog, between you and the customers you attract with your blog, and between you and media folk you'll find to partner with through exposure your blog brings to you.

2 ∼ What Is Branding?

Branding is not advertising, nor publicity, not even general exposure. It is the result of all your efforts, working together, how they coalesce into the public's perception of who you are, what you do. ~ From "Inside Retailing," Carolyn's column for Home Décor Buyer

If you are already well known in your local area or in your niche online, you've probably been diligent about marketing efforts—including publicity—for some time. If you haven't, it is unlikely that you will have the kind of public recognition you'd like. That is why no matter where you are on the path to making your store the purveyor of choice for what you sell, *now* is better than later. Blogging is a big part of that online picture, the powerful interconnected way to promote darn near free.

Even with a background in public relations, I have fallen into many marketing—more precisely, branding—potholes. Ahhh, well, They say experience is the best teacher. Still it will be easier for you if you learn from *my* mistakes rather than going the do-it-yourself-mistakes route.

One of the holes I fell into was leaving myself out of my branding equation. I was at a catalog buying meeting one year when I overhead a woman with a good, strong voice (and a New York accent) telling her friends that she had been doing radio spots for her store. She said, "I was bowled over when a stranger by the pool at the Marriott recognized me by my voice."

The lesson here is that stores don't have voices. You do. Members of your staff do. You and that staff are what make your store truly different from any other. Your job with **branding** is to include enough of you (and them) in your marketing and in all other aspects of your store to make the individuality felt. Not just in your radio spots but in everything you do.

Another aha! moment was when I was using www.vistaprint.com to design business cards. I had trouble getting the cover of an early book I wrote to load. I had seen business cards for real estate professionals that used thumbnail headshots of the agent, so I did the same. Then I muttered to myself, "Well, it's OK because I won't have to do much redesigning when and if I complete another book."

It's the same for retail stores. Of course! When you open another location. When current events dictate changes in your way of doing business. An example: You decide to move your product mix away from expensive home décor to more comforting personal care products during a recession.

Some retailers even end up with stores with different names in different locales. If that should happen, the product mix (if you're listening to your customers) is sure to vary, too. Even Wal-Mart has begun tailoring its mix to individual store locations.

That branding clarity is needed for everything. When you name your Web site. When you name your blog, when you choose a template for your blog, and as you're choosing posts for your blog. Everything needn't revolve around you or even your store's name. Still it is *you* that is the constant.

Here are some aspects of branding you'll want to consider:

- Decide what you want your brand to say. Start with your mission statement. Turn it into a motto or **tagline** that sizzles. You'll jazz up this statement to use in your blog's header.
- Take into consideration what you might do in the future. Even if you're not clairvoyant. That's why department store names like Saks and Macy's have longevity. The owner (original owner) is the focus here and that focus morphs as the store changes over time.
- If you're unsure about your brand (who you are, what your store is) talk to customers and employees. What do they think of when your store name comes up? If you don't already have banners and logos that you can use for your blog, think about them only after you are settled in and as certain as you'll ever be about your focus. If you already have a branding campaign, use this opportunity to get clearer about what it is. You may obtain a free Brand Identity Questionnaire from www.chazdesimone.com to help you clarify your brand. Then an identity design specialist such as Chaz can develop a

professional logo and identity system to indelibly brand your distinct new image.

- When you're making these branding and blog decisions, follow your star. It will be easier to pursue a brand for which you are passionate.
- Don't be afraid to widen your path. You are building a reputation with your brand. You wouldn't want to be known only as honest among dozens of other traits you aspire to.
- Frame yourself as an expert. If you weren't an expert when you first opened your store, you are now. That experience becomes expertise that contributes to the picture you are painting.

Use the concept you have developed everywhere:
- Consider general branding as you design or redesign your Web site and everything else online. Your e-mail signature, the look of your instant messaging. Your Twitter wallpaper, and, yep, your blog.
- Coordinate a "look" for all your paper goods like your stationery but don't forget to carry that through to your checks, your invoices, gift wrap, fliers you use for bag stuffers. Everything.
- Don't forget other stuff that doesn't seem related. You store's sign, display windows, around-the-store signs. Even your voicemail greeting.

So, here's the thing. If you aren't feeling secure on your branding, think about it before you begin to blog. That doesn't mean you must have logos already designed or do it immediately; it does mean that you're pretty clear about the trunk of your tree and its branches so you can apply that clarity to make your entire marketing campaign jell.

3. ♒ Five Essential Steps for Building a Blog

Do-it-yourself on the Web isn't your father's do-it-yourself project; some genius has done lots of the footwork for you. You get to jump in with the creative, fun part.

Blog building proves that there is some whiz kid behind every genius, especially when that genius is the proverbial "us." Once you start you'll see how easy it is because of some **content management service** that someone else designed. And often it is offered to you free. Guys and gals at Google have made blogging especially easy with blogspot.com (also called blogger.com for reasons only known to Google!). With it you can start a blog with five (only five!) essential steps.

You start with your free Google account. You may already have one. If you do, the words "My Account" will appear as a link on Google's homepage. It's in blue in the top right corner. If not, use a link on that page to set up your account.

1. Once you have an account, you'll find a whole bunch of services that Google offers—also free. Many of them are miracles disguised as **links**, but right now

we're only interested in the little orange **icon** (or logo) with the "Blogger" link next to it. Click on that link.

2. Find the link that says "create a blog." Click.

3. The first prompt will ask you to name your blog. Choose wisely. Go back to the section before this on **branding**; read it all the way through so you don't choose a name for your blog that is too narrowly focused or too broad. (For now, ignore the "advanced option" section.)

4. Next choose a template, something simple. Play with colors that fit your branding campaign, the looks of your store or Web site. Avoid dark backgrounds. They are hard to read.

5. Your next window says "Start Blogging." That may be oversimplified, but it's close. Take your time to browse the "settings" and "layout" tabs. Don't worry about making a mistake. Play with the provided windows until you feel secure. You can always make changes later.

See how easy that was! As you move forward in putting new "segments" or "**gadgets**" on your blog, know that nothing is chiseled in stone. Anything you do can be undone. I started a blog when I wrote *A Retailer's Guide to Frugal In-Store Promotions: How To Increase Profits and Spit in the Eyes of Economic Downturns with Thrifty Events and Sales Techniques* as a tool to help retailers but also, frankly, to help them see that they need to continue their education in all matters retailing. With my books and booklets and those of others. With blogs and articles on the Web. With tradeshow buyer education programs. That blog is at www.frugalretailing.blogspot.com.

As I built the blog, I made notes for the step-by-step instructions for this book and it was even easier than I remembered. You can delete and start over or keep tweaking until you have your very first attempt just the way you want it. It costs you nothing to enjoy the process but the time you might otherwise spend playing online solitaire.

If you are not a freshman computer user and have a Web site of your own, consider incorporating your blog into your existing site's format. The frequent fresh content of a blog makes the search engines happy. It will make you happy, too, when you see your site move up in the online ratings.

If you don't already have a Web site, don't have anyone to help you add a blog to your Web site, or you just want to blog the easy way, start blogging right now at Blogger.com using the steps listed above. That's where I started, and I still use it because it's so simple, so frugal (free) and because my subscriber list now has so many people on it I'm loathe to switch to another format. Phyllis Zimbler Miller is a tech-minded friend with a company called Miller Mosaic. She started with Blogspot.com, too. She hasn't switched her blog to her own site yet but she says she eventually will.

Hint: You can see from the five steps above that you can start a blog on Blogger.com in less than five minutes. Adding some of the extra features that blogger.com makes available for your blog may take somewhat longer, but you add them as needs arise and as you get more comfortable with the blogging process.

Other places you might choose to house your blog are www.typepad.com and www.wordpress.com. You choose where your blog will live the way you would choose a new home—based on the features you like best. Or you choose Blogspot because I told you it is easy and sufficient for most retailers' needs.

4. ⌁ The Why-I-Should Blog and How-to-Find-Time Chapter

> Blogging is like picking strawberries. We fill our baskets more quickly if we take the time to push aside the leaves.

I want to dispel concerns you have about blogging so we'll talk about why blogging works for retailers and how you find time for yet one more task.

I know. You'd rather be selling. I could point out that blogging *is* selling but what would be the use? I know what you mean.

But think about it. You have the same problem with other aspects of marketing and you somehow make time or get help. They include things that take a considerable chunk of your budget, like producing catalogs, in-store promotions, and advertising on radio, TV, and in print. Blogging is better. Except for the time, blogging is free. And blogging is far more connected (read that interactive) with a broader audience than anything we've ever experienced with **old media**.

THE ADVANTAGES TO BLOGGING ARE MANY. Here are the reasons you should blog instead of working at many promotions that may not be as effective:

33

- Blogging is creative and that's right up your alley. I don't know of a retailer who doesn't have a bit of the artist in her or him.
- Blogging is a good way to build customer loyalty and to produce sales.
- Blogging helps build name recognition for your store and makes it easier for your customers to find you with search engines.

> Hint: Blogger / Blogspot is an entity of Google and I believe that is a big reason that material on that **content service** appears so quickly in the Google search engine. It is also why the Google **alerts** for that material come to people using that service so quickly.

- From the information in the Five-Easy-Steps Chapter, you will see that blogging is an easy—repeat easy—way to build a presence on search engines. Many who will be checking on you in the future will be impressed by an active blogger and by a store with a huge footprint on these same engines.
- Blogs let your voice come through to your customers and that is an important aspect of great **branding**. Many times the customers you reach with your blog are the ones you haven't met because you aren't in the store when they are. That means enhanced loyalty over a broader customer base. Customers who search for subjects online

(your store does have lots of subjects—they're your products and services) get a feeling of who you are by what you choose to feature on your blog and how you choose to tell about those things.

- Did I mention that blogging, except for your time, is free?

KEEPING YOUR BLOGGING TIME CORRALLED is important to any retailer.

You've probably heard that you must blog every day. Of course you don't. And there are no blog-frequency cops. Nevertheless the rule-of-thumb is that you post frequently and that takes time. Here are some time-saving ways for you to keep an active blog and keep your time expenditure within reason:

Use guest bloggers. You offer someone the opportunity to write one or several guest posts on a subject that fits with your blog. Asking others to guest blog isn't only a good way to save time, it's a great way to network. Your guest may then promote your blog and, by extension, your store. You can handle the guest-blogger process two ways. They can submit directly to you and you do the posting. I like this method because you can better control your blog and the editing process. But in the "settings" feature of your blog you'll find a feature called "permissions" that allows the guest to do their own posting.

Hint: You may also guest blog for other bloggers. This will get you (and your blog, Web site, and store) in front of other audiences. If you include links in your guest-blogger credits (sometimes called a **tagline**), some people will click on them and be carried back to your other online entities. These active links are known as **incoming links** (also called **back links**). Search engines love links that lead to your blog! The little Google spiders that search for such things think you are important if your blog has a lot of them. They then raise your blog in the search engine rankings.

Get partners for your blog. Find compatible fellow retailers, vendors, representatives, or customers who will agree to write one or two posts a week. Then you'd only be responsible for an equivalent number of posts. When folks combine their talents and time, the power of the project increases incrementally both in terms of promoting the blog and in the sheer posting power. Search engines love blogs with lots of new content. The drawback is that the spotlight may not shine only on your store, though I can see how it still might if your partner is an employee or a customer.

Hint: You may be wondering why you'd want to share your blog with a fellow retailer. Sure, you'd need to be selective, but I can see a grand partnership between a yarn shop and a bead shop. Metaphorically, the bead shop embellishes the yarn shop and the yarn shop provides the fabric for the bead shop.

Recycle articles, tips, bargains, and anything else you can think of from the other things you do—some of them from past years. Your images can be the same ones you use in your catalogs. Your articles are often the same ones you use in your newsletters or on your Web site, but spaced so they don't appear in the same month. Everything on your blog doesn't have to be new or exclusive, and everything you write for your blog may be cycled back to those other venues.

Use the carnival concept. A **carnival** is a kind of blog that lists the best blog posts in the blogosphere—but only those related to your blog's focus. You group the **links** to those blogs along with a little synopsis of each in a post. Some blogs post nothing but carnivals. Tony Eldridge, a former marketing professional, blogs on book marketing (blog.marketingtipsforauthors.com/) and he posts a carnival on Fridays. He finds great posts by subscribing to related blogs. Carnivals save writing time, but you may spend more time reading other people's blogs to find good content.

Outsource your blogging to a writer who is familiar with blogs. He or she might charge per blog or per month for so many blog posts. Obviously your blog won't be free if you choose to do this, but you'll balance that expense against what blogging space would cost if you were paying for display advertising. Factor in the value of the time you would save, too.

All you need do is supply the information for each blog. After your new freelance helper becomes familiar with your store, she may come up with ideas of her own and thus expand what you could do yourself. Two such writers are Mindy Lawrence (mplcreative1@aol.com) and Terese Morrow (keybusinesspartners@yahoo.com).

If you're better at talking than writing, use videos on your blog. Talking takes less time than writing even for professional writers. If you are self conscious about your writing it may feel more comfortable to talk into a Webcam. So you film yourself talking rather than spend your time writing. Tony Eldridge is a marketer who often uses videos as teaching tools. Learn five ways to use videos on you blog from this expert at:

> http://blog.marketingtipsforauthors.com/2009/0
> 8/5-ways-to-use-video-on-your-site-and.html

Blogging is important. It's also not nearly as scary or time consuming as many think. So let's get moving.

5. ≈ There's No Such Thing as Bloggers' Block

Blogging is like life. It grows organically, invisibly as you move through each day.

Writers worry about writers' block; retailers worry about bloggers' block. Lots of retailers let that concern keep them from starting a blog. What to write about! Really! What *do* you write about? Reassuringly, there are only a few guidelines and tons of material.

To attract and keep readers, a blog must include practical information that others can use. It is not that hard and the process of doing it helps a store owner focus on his or her store's strengths and the aspects of his operation that make it unique.

As it turns out, it is easier for some kinds of stores than others, but it's possible for all them for they all share some qualities by virtue of their being stores.

BLOG-ONLY BARGAINS may be the most natural subjects for most retailers to come up with. From a marketing standpoint, it is a good idea to feature a new special each week; regular features—especially ones that help people save money—encourage your blog visitors to subscribe to your posts so that they won't miss a single one. In fact, occasionally suggest that they subscribe. Point them to the subscribe feature on your blog. Learn more about ways to do this in Chapter Eight.

> Hint: You know your own profit margins, your own inventory. Those are the elements of any special you consider. Once the popularity of your blog-only offers grows, watch for closeouts from your vendors, and attend surplus tradeshows for items with a high perceived value and low cost.

A CARNIVAL OF THINGS TO BLOG ABOUT is appearing under the stupendous *Your Blog, Your Business* tent today. Here are things that most or all stores have in common that are supremely bloggable:

- Your employees. New ones. Employees getting awards. Employees celebrating long term anniversaries with you. Employees who come up with ideas to improve your operations. You can see how being featured on your blog might work as an inducement for staff members to be more loyal and more creative.
- Your merchandise. New lines. Old lines. New shipments. The licensed artists for these lines. You might even interview those licensed artists. What a coup to get Kincade or Tony Evans of Fusion Z to agree to an interview. Really something to blog about! And something to tweet about, too. Tweets will lead folks to your blog posts!
- The parts of retailing that the public finds exotic. New window displays. The buying

process and, yes, the traveling you do as part of that buying. Who says you couldn't talk about not only the new products you find at the National Stationery Show but also the $25. mocha martini you had on the roof of the Marriott in Times Square.

- Yourself. If you spend time in the store, you will be of interest to your customers. You won't need to share your religion or your politics (unless you have a store associated with your views on religion or politics), but your customers may get a kick out of sharing a birthday celebration or hearing you rant about a shopping experience you found miserable or one you found so wonderful it had your head spinning.

- Anything that is in the news that relates to your store or product lines. If you carry toys, product recall information would benefit them. If you institute something like a solar-heated water system, that news fits with reports on the environment that occur almost every day of the year. If you your store is in Vermont and you're having an especially warm spring that brings in lots of customers, that can be blogged about. An especially icy week is an occasion for a free-shipping-with-phone-orders-over-$25. offer.

- Talk about retailing in general. You think people aren't interested? How many people have said, "Oh, I'd love to have a store like this!" to you in the last year. Generally, people are very interested in what retailers are doing and the choices they make.

- Every store has vendors. Get them involved. **Link** to the articles on their blogs and Web sites. Ask them to contribute in some way to your blog with special purchases or written material.
- Get specific about your products. If you carry porcelain, blog on how it is made. If you carry patio furniture, explain how one of your lines is made with forest-friendly woods.
- Talk about how you serve your customers. Things like your rewards card, your layaway plan, and your gift wrap.
- Talk about your coming events. Arrange specials and give-aways tailored to spark interest for your events. See *A Retailer's Guide to Frugal In-Store Promotions: How To Increase Profits and Spit in the Eyes of Economic Downturns with Thrifty Events and Sales Techniques* for tons of event ideas and related in-store promotions.

On their blogs retailers may also:
- Review books that relate to their products or their business philosophy.
- Let readers follow along with the process of a new expansion or new-store project.
- Create contests for merchandise prizes.
- Let customers submit material for blogs. Make a contest of that, too.
- Encourage your employees to submit articles or anecdotes about your store.
- Quote from blogs and Web sites with a focus related to yours. I've seen blog posts that are

nothing more than one great inspirational quotation.

> Hint: There is a free-use clause in copyright law. For reviews, essays, and articles, you can quote short pieces from other works at no charge and, yes, without permission. Some online bookstores allow quotes in blurbs of up to 25 words. It's easy to find interesting quotes from artists, celebrities, and people in the business world. Quotations can be seasonal, about the retailing climate, about shopping, about fashion and trends.

Glean ideas as you go about your day. Everything you do may spark an idea for a blog or other marketing entity. Carry a notebook and pencil with you everywhere.

Examine your own store for a handle on subjects to blog about, for ideas for future media releases, and for feature ideas you could pitch to editors. There is no point in doing this exercise twice or three times. Let's get organized and make one such thorough examination a month work for more than just our blogs.

Similarly, watch for ideas in the larger world about you. TV is good. Especially the ads; can you somehow tie a blog to "Dancing with the Stars" and still keep your focus? When you read the daily newspapers or watch the news, jot down ideas on how you might relate your blog content to current events. When I don't have writing equipment, I tear pages and ragged little clippings out of magazines, newspapers, and even junk mail.

As you wander down the aisles of a gift show, you ask yourself "What are the angles—right here—that I can exploit?"

I know you already take busman's holidays. How could you not? Ditto for busman's shopping sprees. To the grocery store. To your favorite charity's second-hand-rose shop. To the mall. You become a reporter, use the same power of observation you use in selecting product. Use that notebook to take notes on everything, but especially blog ideas.

6. ≋ E-Gifts: Combine Your Expertise and Your Freebies

> It's human nature. We want free stuff for ourselves but, when it comes to business, hesitate to give anything away. We need to change our thinking to "Free is the gift that keeps giving back."

Bloggers (and retailers in general) are often confounded by how to offer something free to their subscribers and visitors without breaking the bank.

Sure we want to offer something free. A freebie might encourage people to:
- To subscribe to our blogs.
- To visit our stores.
- To buy something else.
- To spread the word about our blog.
- To support our other **social networking** efforts.
- To become involved even though they don't live in our defined market area.

Just any freebie won't do, though. At least some of the freebies we offer should:
- Ship at no cost, i.e. get delivered electronically rather than by post.

- Have a high perceived value.
- Offer information that will encourage sales and inspire loyalty.
- Last a long time and contribute to your brand.
- Enhance your image as an expert in your field.

Here's what meets all those requirements. Books. Not paperback or hardcover books (though they may be produced that way, too). No. E-books. Maybe not even books, but booklets or whitepapers that can be distributed online.

There is a section in *Frugal and Focused Tweeting for Retailers: Tweaking Your Tweets and Other Tips for Integrating Your Social Media* that talks about using printed matter (read that *information*!) to grow your online influence.

Sometimes you can get electronic booklets from your vendors. Or you can get content from them that you can turn into e-books yourself. As an example, your customers and future customers want to know more about the licensed artists whose work appears on some of your card lines. They want to know how to plan their wedding invitations without committing a social faux pas. Of course, you can also write from your own solid base of expertise. Whatever you think your customers want. You know them better than anyone else. Choose a topic that will shine a spotlight on you and your store.

These booklets can be inducements, but they can also be given away with no strings attached. Make sure there is enough in each one to frame your store as the go-to place to get products and information. There should be references to you in the body of the booklet, ads for your services and products in the back. Booklets on how people can protect their fragile home décor items from the ravishes of earthquakes will stay in customers' computers for a very long time, or get printed out to put with their emergency supplies. Or be a great community service—either as a paper pamphlet or as an e-booklet—for Kiwanis or your Chamber of Commerce to distribute.

If you print the booklet as a paperback, let your blog drive customers to your store to pick their books up in person or encourage out-of-the-area customers to buy something to get their book shipped to them with their order. Your book could also be tucked into shipments going to customers who live in another state as a little extra surprise.

Go to CreateSpace.com and poke around. You'll see that the cost for a promotion item like this is virtually free for the basic service and, once published, the cost of copies can be very low when compared to most advertising costs. If you don't feel you have the expertise, hire a consultant like me to help with your first booklet and you'll feel comfortable doing it on your own ever after that.

7. ≋ Blog Interaction: Building Relationships

Think of your blog as a modern-day telephone that no one ever gets turned away from with a busy tone. It's on-demand communication at its best.

A blog is intended to create relationships between the blogger and the blog's readers. You encourage that by asking for comments from readers or by asking questions in your blog post.

Enable the comments feature of your blog so that your readers can ask questions and contribute ideas (and, yes, do a little subtle promoting of their own). Find the tool for this feature under "settings" on your Blogger **dashboard**.

Peter Bowerman, author of the Well-Fed Writer series of books, once told me that to blog and expound and expound and blog is losing the interactive quality that blogging is meant to foster. He ends almost every one of his posts with a question.

Here are some ways to get some interaction going.
- Ask questions in your blog.
- Ask for submissions for guest posts.

- Hold contests of all kinds. For merchandise. For the privilege of being published on your blog.
- Give freebies. As an example, you offer a whitepaper if they join you on your other **social networks**.

> Hint: About that last bullet. A blog is not a stand-alone entity. It is part of the wider world of the Web. The more you acknowledge its interactivity with **links** and connections to your other **social networks**, the more traffic you build for all of them. You'll find an entire chapter that gives specific ideas for this kind of online bonding in my book *Frugal and Focused Tweeting*. You'll also find more ways to get people to come to your blog in the next chapter.

8. ≋ The Blogging Law of Attraction

Attracting people to our blogs reminds me of the little white and black Scottie dog magnets I once played with. They pushed one another away or pulled one another together, depending on how we played the game.

Blogs aren't like the proverbial *Field of Dreams* in which you "build it and they will come." In spite of the amazing interconnectedness of the Web and all the things you can do to get people to come visit, read what you say, get hooked on what you can do for them, and maybe even eventually buy your merchandise—a blog still needs you to promote it.

Most people think of **search** engines as the easiest and best way to get readership so they spend lots of time submitting their blog address to those engines and directories. Forget it. That's the old way, and I only mention it because retailers new to blogging may run across an old article on the Web that tells them it's essential.

In his whitepaper "Planning for Success: How to Build a Professional Blog," Chris Garrett, who wrote the book *Problogger* with Darren Rowse, says:

"You may wonder why I haven't suggested submitting to search engines or directories. In fact you do not need to submit to search engines; get **inbound links** and [people] will find you. Directories are a mixed bag. I rarely see any traffic from them and their influence in search has waned."

COLLABORATE WITH OTHER BLOGGERS to promote your blog. Because the world is littered with competing signals these days, it is almost impossible for any promotional undertaking to do well without purposely letting people know about it. Here are ways you might publicize your blog other than the ones we've already talked about.

Give away breaking news. Let's say the Japanese have come up with a breakthrough in producing porcelain that will reduce its cost by 20% and you get a media release to that effect. You decide you're going to write about that in you blog as it relates to your porcelain products and the present economic situation. If you know of influential bloggers in your area of expertise (and you should make it your business to know!), give them a heads up that you'll be posting the news the next day and that they have first dibs on linking to it. In effect, you're giving these few bloggers a chance at breaking the news first; something they will love because breaking news is probably what made these bloggers influential to begin with.

Join a group of bloggers. Many people join a small circle of bloggers who agree to visit each other's blogs and leave comments whenever there's a new post. This strategy works well because comments attract more comments, and these fellow commenters may become good networking partners.

Trade articles with other bloggers. Your guest blogger gets to include a nice credit line with a link to his blog and other **social networks** and you get to do the same for her when you allow her to use one of yours.

Start a blogger group. It's a little like the guest-blogger idea but more organized and more frequent: Group members feature one another in your blogs complete with logos, storefront pictures, and headshots of the store owners. These may be interviews they conduct with you via e-mail or articles you write and contribute as a guest blogger. They showcase your expertise (say the resurgence of home sewing since the recession because you sell craft supplies) and you do something similar for them (they write about how sewing machines have improved in the last decade because they manufacture sewing machines).

If you keep accruing new members with something in common, this exchange cycle can grow without ever duplicating an interview, article, or other kind of post. Each time you are featured on a new blog, you reach a new audience.

LET WEB ENTITIES ATTRACT READERS in lots of different ways. Today bloggers use Technorati, Digg, Del.icio.us, Pingomatic, and other platforms as the workhorses for their blogs. You do that by installing **widgets** designed to let your visitors share your brilliant blogs with their **social networks**. To install them on your blog, you use **RSS feeds**. (See Chapter Ten for more on feeds and **HTML** codes.)

Once you're familiar with blogging, reading books like *Problogger* to help you disseminate the news about your posts with helps from these free (but relatively advanced) services. Until then, attract traffic in simple ways:

- Choose tags or **labels** (otherwise known as **keywords**) and put them in the designated window just beneath the **posting window** on the page you use to enter new posts. It's easy. They are just the words that people will most likely search for. For example, if people are searching for more on blogging, they might search on "blogs," "writing blogs," "building a blog," "starting a blog," "blogs for retailers," "blogging for retailers," "writing for blogs," "online promotion," "online promotion for retailers," and so on. Those are the **keywords** or **tags** I would enter in that window if I were posting any part of this booklet on my blog.
- Find others who blog on similar subjects and ask them to trade **links** with you.
- Include your blog address and benefits for reading it in your e-mail signature.
- Include a **social networking** page on your Web site so people can learn more about you. Don't just list the **links** to your Facebook, Twitter, and blog; add a little note about the benefits

customers will get if they take a minute to click through to those sites. Even if your blog is on your Web site you can provide an **internal link** from many places on your site that takes your customer to the page your blog is on.

- Submit your blog for awards. Nominate your own blog for a Blog of the Day award (blogofthedayawards.blogspot.com). Learn what trade associations and local business groups offer in the way of rewarding savvy promoters. When your blog gets recognition, promote that win with as many other marketing methods from this book that are suitable (and most of them will be!).

   Hint: When you win an award, send out a media release to your media contact list, and post the award logo on your blog, your Web site, and in your newsletter. Learn more about building contact lists in *Frugal and Focused Tweeting* and later in this chapter as well. Find a sample media release in Appendix Four of this book.

- Mention your blog on your other social networks. *Frugal and Focused Tweeting for Retailers* includes a whole chapter on how to grab down the power of Internet by **linking** one online entity with another.

   Hint: Do this connecting in a way that gives your audience information they want or need. Don't make it only about you, your store, or your blog, but about the needs of your customer.

- Get people to subscribe to your blog right from your blog page. Blogspot offers **gadgets**—they are easy-to-use techno gizmos that do most of the work for any given blog project for you. One of them sends your blog directly to readers' e-mail boxes automatically. Those readers must sign up for it (in tech lingo, they "**opt in**.") Find it under "gadgets" on your "layout" page. When they subscribe (opt in) their little picture or **avatar** will appear on your blog. Lots of people who enjoy the Web or are great Web marketers like seeing their own pictures or logos in these sections of blogs, so offering them the opportunity to be part of your blog is further encouragement for them to keep your blogs coming to them automatically.

> Hint: Increase your chance of letting others find you when they type in words related to your blog on a search engine like Google. One way to do that is to spread your name, Web address, and blog address around on other blogs by leaving comments on blogs you visit. Your comments should add something to the conversation and keep the interests of the blogger's audience in mind. You don't usually have to include your site information in your signature because when you log onto the site, those invisible blog services do some of this work for you. They automatically link the name you used to log onto the blog service back to your Web site. But you should do even more. Leave your blog address (if different from your Web site address) with your signature or a little

information on your next in-store or online event. Something like this:

Very best,
Susan Marshall
Blogging knitting and other handcraft tips at KnittingforYou.blogspot.com.

A FEW LITTLE SECRETS to help you attract readers to your blog and keep them coming back involve writing and formatting. Not to worry. That doesn't mean you must become a full-blown journalist. Here are a few simple tricks:

Headlines (or titles) of your blog will appear in the search engines. If you keep them punchy, you will keep them fun and that attracts readers. You do that by:

- Using active and unlikely verbs. For instance, "Corral" may work better than "keep" in a headline.
- Use numbers in headlines. It's been proven that people are more likely to read titles like "Three Easy Ways to Avoid Water Spots on Your Crystal."
- Use teasers like: "What's the One Thing People Forget When Trying on Bathing Suits?"

If you don't already, begin to pay attention to the headlines on the magazines and tabloids stowed near the checkout at grocery stores. The *National Enquirer* editors are masters at the tease. Besides, it's a more productive activity than getting steamed up about the long check-out lines.

Formatting is important, too. Make whatever you have to say easy to read.

- Use white space when you can.
- Use bullets to guide the readers' eyes down your copy.
- Keep your blogs short for the most part. It's best to stay under 700 words if you can.
- Use **links** whenever you mention anything that can be linked. To other blogs, to the Web sites of organizations or any other entity, to videos you want your readers to see and on and on.
- Use tons of images. You already know how pictures sell merchandise. But include shots of you, your staff, your store, your windows, your customers, your contest prizes. Some bloggers do whole blog posts using nothing but images and brief descriptive passages.

Writing style can keep people coming back to your blog, too. Humor is the number one way to do that, but a fun, colloquial style will, too.

Of course, there's always content. Content reigns supreme. You knew that because you don't want to waste your time, either. See Appendix Two for some great writing brush-up aids.

USE PROMOTION TOOLS YOU'VE ALWAYS USED. The tried and true should never be discarded.

- Use your own contact list. In *A Retailer's Guide to Frugal In-Store Promotions,* I talk about the importance of list building. Your own personal list of contacts and your store's customer list will be your first and most important resources to build readership of your blog, and growing that list should be an ongoing project for you from the first moment you decide to go into retailing.

- Include your blog address on your business card, your checks, your class handouts if you teach, the fliers you stuff in your shopping bags, and in the credits of the articles you write.
- Use events.
- Use all your **old media** methods. Just be sure they're updated to include information about your **new media** blog and other **social networks**.

Simply put, make promoting your blog part of the work you do each day. That way it takes little or no extra time for promotion but flows seamlessly into all the things you do to promote your store.

9 ≈ Now You've Got 'Em, Convert Them to Customers

Attracting customers is no different than making friends. Let them know you have their interests at heart and they'll come running to you.

Aside from getting people to come to your blog, you want them to know about you (and ideally, for you to know about them). To do that you:

- Use a mission statement of sorts near the blog header. Even though you can cast your imagination net far and wide for subjects on which to blog, your visitor wants to know what the focus of the blog is. If they can't immediately determine that, they may go elsewhere. To put that statement on your blog, go to your "layout" page, click on the "settings" tab, and type your message into the box that says "Description."

  Hint: That statement should feel light and caring. It shouldn't sound like a letter full of business-ese.

- Activate a live **link** for everything you write about. Doing so is a *service*. These links are what visitors use to easily learn more on subjects that you talk about. If your blog doesn't make that effortless, they may move on to a blog that does. So you include live links to names of organizations, places where you took quotations from, the Web sites of people you mention and on and on. (You make those words live by using the little world-shaped **icon** you find in the tool bar at the top of your blog's **post window**.)

- At the bottom of each post, include a blogger credit. A credit (sometimes called a resource box or **tagline**) is a mini biography with your name, your store name, and **links** to the buy pages on your blog or your Web site. This mini bio can be in smaller typeface, set apart with dashes or a line of tildes. Most blog services, including blogger.com, let you automate this process. When you're in your blogger **dashboard** (sort of the home page to your blog or blogs), go to the "settings" tab and then the "formatting" tab. Scroll down to the bottom where you'll find a "post template" window in which you type in your personal data and links. Once entered, you never have to revisit it unless you must change links, open another store, or think of a better way to word the credit. Because this credit gets automatically added to your blog window every time you post, this one feature will save you oodles of time.

- Include information that propels your visitors to visit other projects you are participating in on the Web. The side panels (columns) on the right or left of your blog and the areas at the bottom of your blog are your little workhorses. They should include:

- **Widgets** (little click-through logos that take readers to where they can buy your special offerings or where they can find your other **social networks**).
- **Labels** (an index of sorts) is a single entry in one of the columns of your blog. It will appear either on the right or left, depending on the template you chose. It's like a little index that lists topics you've discussed on your blog; visitors use it to research subjects that interest them. On my TheNewBookReview.blogspot.com, you'll see I provide labels (essentially **keywords**) so that readers can find reviews of genres that interest them. Most likely visitors won't already know the title of a book, but they will know they want to see reviews of books in the category of "Nonfiction: Business." Your blog would most likely include labels for your brand name products, and for your services.
- Lists may be added as well. You'll want a list of the awards your blog and/or store(s) have won, and a list of your coming events.

Hint: Look into Google's calendar feature to help you with lists of your coming events. It makes life easy. I fill in the calendar once, and it appears on my blog, my Web site or about any other place I tell it I want it to go, and it disappears once the date of the event is past with no help from me. It's super easy and saves lots of time. You'll use **HTML** code provided by Google to install it on your blog.

- A video or **podcast**. These elements might feature you explaining how to plan a wedding or how to make a beaded purse. You can also use others' videos that relate to your material, especially those of your savvy suppliers. You might rebroadcast a podcast that a radio host has made of an interview with you. Including an element like this will impress your visitors, and radio hosts who see you promoting their efforts and might then ask you back.
- A resource box that gives tips or information that your visitors are likely to use. I use little tip boxes on every page of my Web site to entice visitors to browse through the entire site. On my War Peace Tolerance blog, I include a list of resources

where readers can help troops at no cost or with very little money. It, too, is a Blogger / Blogspot blog (warpeacetolerance.blogspot.com). Your resource box might list **links** to your famous brand suppliers' fan pages on Facebook.

- A **blog roll** in which you list other blogs where your visitors can find material related to yours.

- A subscription **link** or **widget** that lets your visitors sign up to get your new posts automatically. I mention this feature in other places in this book, too, because it is so important. There are several ways to do this. Blogger offers a **gadget** accessed from your **dashboard**. Click on the "layout" tab. There you can "add a gadget." One of these is "subscription links." It says "Let your readers easily subscribe to your blog with popular **feed readers**." (See Chapter Ten for more on feed readers.)

- A **trailer** is a visual you might consider. These are not same as the videos we talked about earlier, but more like what you see before the feature film in theaters. They say a picture is worth a thousand words. If you'd like to outsource one for your blog, Reno Lovison produced the trailer I use on my blog at frugalretailing.blogspot.com. He is not only an expert at producing trailers, he has a marketing and retail background that he puts to good use on your behalf. To learn more about him go to http://renoweb.net/.

In the blog posts themselves, don't be afraid to mention your store, your products, and yourself. Include a live link to a sales page on your Web site whenever you can work it into your copy. If these references are an integral part of your content, they will be viewed as a service, not as blatant marketing or an imposition.

10 ≈ Now You've Got 'Em, Keep Them Coming Back

A blog is like a well-planned holiday party. Inspire your guests. Feed them well. Send them home with a favor. Lo! They will want to come back next year.

Think of a person who has shown an interest in your blog as a treasure to be stashed away for safe keeping and then used in ways that will benefit you both. You have more control over that process if you encourage them to access your blog on a regular basis.

You do that by letting people sign up or subscribe to get an e-mail containing each of your new blog posts or an e-mail with a link to your blog post:

1. The easiest way is to use Blogger.com's "add a gadget" feature. Or you can choose another service like Feedblitz.com.
2. Use **RSS** (Real Simple Syndication) so people can get your blog fed into their **feed readers**. RSS is probably called "syndication" because it is related to syndicated columns in newspapers. That is, it lets one article be seen in many places just like a syndicated column or comic strip that appears in our daily paper and many others across the country, sometimes the world.

"Readers" are techie systems that let your visitors compile information they will want to . . . well, *read*. For example, if your visitor uses Google's reader, he clicks on the RSS link on your blog and directs it to feed the headlines of your new posts complete with **links** right to his Google reader. It's like spoon feeding a baby. Then, when he's ready to catch up on his reading, he goes to his Google reader. There he'll find all the reading he's signed up for waiting for him. Thus, **RSS** and readers make it "really, really simple" for your loyal visitors to know you've posted something on your blog. (For more on RSS feeds and other advanced blogging techniques consider one of MaAnna Stephenson's books. She has written three RSS feed e-books. Each gives details necessary to use RSS on different platforms, including Blogger, WordPress.com, and WordPress.org.

The buy page for Stephenson's books is: http://www.justthefaqs.net/buybooks.shtml.

> Hint: To learn more about how these subscription feeds (and other elements of a blog) work, subscribe to other people's blogs and analyze each for its use of gadgets including **RSS feeds**. Notice where they place their Feedblitz subscription service, how they present their blog rolls, how they use videos, how often they post, etc. Find a couple of mine at www.sharingwithwriters.blogspot.com and www.frugalretailing.blogspot.com. You can always unsubscribe after you've gotten the gist of it, but it's better if you hang around for more ideas for your business and your writing. You *are* a writer now that you blog!

11 ≋ Is It Ever "A Wrap?"

"It's a wrap" signals achievement of a goal in the entertainment industry. "Wrap it up," signals the close of a sale for retailers. A successfully installed blog is a "wrap" that never stops needing attention.

Blogging on your own blog(s) and as a guest blogger on other peoples' blogs are creative and effective ways to attract customers who, at first, may be only readers. Your effort may result in an instant conversion. Or it may not. In any case, I want to reiterate that finding paying customers is certainly a goal but not the only benefit of blogging.

I've given you an overview of the important points of blogging in the service of retail marketing. There are whole books written on blogging in general, but none I know of help you specifically with the needs of a retailer. Still. even with practical retail-oriented guidance, you may want to measure your success yourself.

MEASURING YOUR BLOGGING SUCCESS can't be done in terms of traceable sales. You're used to that. Oh, occasionally you'll run a blog-only bargain and be able to see results—perhaps not specific ones, but at least indications. Other than that you may rely on a Word or Excel graph that shows a constant uptick indicating you're doing a whole battery of things right, but they still won't point to your blog and shout "Hooray! You did it!"

I believe in anecdotal results. If someone tells you they love your blog, that person is one of a large number who thinks the same thing. If someone offers you a tip for improving it, he probably isn't the only one who had the same idea; he's the only one verbal and caring enough (or crotchety enough) to express it to you.

There are a few more formal ways to get meaningful input:

- Sign up for Google Analytics or another similar service and install it on your blog using the "gadgets" tool for **HTML** code we talked about before.
- Check the statistics on your Web site and blog before you start a specific blog campaign. Then check afterward for spikes in your visitor numbers.
- Use these statistics to tell you which posts are getting the most interest. Think about why that might be. Was it the headline? The subject matter? Or was it the promotion you did for those posts (like a mention on LinkedIn) that made them so popular?
- Learn how your visitors are finding you (or rather, where on the Web they are coming

from). Google Analytics has a great pie chart that gives you this information.

> Hint: Analytics has a cool map that lets you see what part of the world your visitors hail from. I love this one. Watching it is a bit like an ongoing geography lesson and it's a visual that emphasizes the encompassing power of the Internet.

When you are evaluating your blog, don't use the number of comments from visitors who come to your blog as a reliable indication of interest. Unless you blog's about something extremely controversial or you are especially skilled at asking questions to entice readers to leave comments, rarely do they take the time to write you a note, much less a chatty one.

Tony Eldridge offers tips on how to measure your success on his marketing blog:

> http://blog.marketingtipsforauthors.com/2009/07/8-ways-to-track-your-website-and-blogs.html.

Using these tips will help you get the idea that you are doing something right so you can get better at doing it.

You'll find more on using statistics in my book *Frugal and Focused Tweeting for Retailers.*

You can see that even these statistics aren't foolproof methods of measuring success. They never tell the full story. The acquisition of one great customer is by far more important to your bottom line than a huge number of hits on your blog. Having said that, if you can convert a huge number of hits to a few more paying customers, you have indeed hit blogger pay dirt.

If Google's Analytics is new to you or you'd like to pick up a few new tricks, you'll like:

http://marketingtipsforauthors.com/Frugal/GAVi deo/FrugalTipintro2ga.html.

It's Tony Eldridge's video introduction to Analytics.

Remember the important first step—start blogging! If it will help your mindset, think of it as a hobby. Once started, you'll learn and refine until your blog is a full-fledged marketing powerhouse.

APPENDIX ONE: YOUR GLOSSARY OF BLOGGING TERMS

Alerts are services offered by many online entities, especially Google Alerts. GA is designed to let people know when they have been mentioned anywhere on the Web. Users sign up through Google Accounts and choose **keywords** that they think are pertinent to their business or current project. Alerts help with marketing, with remembering to send thank yous, with research and more. They get sent right to your e-mailbox.

Avatar is the little identifying symbol or icon that visually illustrates who you are on the Web. Think of it the way you would the signs used by merchants in medieval times when the masses couldn't read. They're instant identification for who you are and what you do.

Blog roll is a list of **links** to other blogs on your blog. It is a service to your readers. The list often includes blogs with a slightly different focus than yours.

Branding is a marketing concept that means finding just the right flavor, just the right message for your store so it can be reflected in everything you do from your motto to the colors and font you use in your printed and online materials. Learn more about branding in *A Retailer's Guide to Frugal In-Store Promotions.*

Carnival is a format some blogs use all the time, others use only one day a week. It is simply the assembling of lots of **links** (along with a little description or pitch about the subject matter of each) to blogs and Web sites you think will interest your reader, much like a carnival gathers fun activities all into one place.

Content management system (or **CMS**) is tech talk for the programs that operate invisibly behind blogs. They make blogging super easy for retailers. Most visitors to blogs have no idea about these brains behind the blog.

Dashboard is the screen you look at to help you steer your blog (and some other online entities). It's like a map with **links** to the **gadgets**, settings and other puzzle pieces that are behind what your blog looks like to visitors.

Feed readers are places online that list the reading people would like to do at their leisure. For a blog to be listed on a person's reader (or readers), they must first register with the reader service and then **opt in** or subscribe to blogs or newsletters that interest them. As bloggers, we hope to offer enough benefits that many will want to keep up with the wisdom (and bargains!) that we proffer.

Gadgets is a term used for all the neat stuff that the bright techies at Blogger / Blogspot have developed, stuff that let's you do amazing things with a blog easily.

HTML is the code you can use to feed (see **RSS feed** and **feed reader** in this glossary) Twitter (and other things) to your blog and other online entities like Facebook. Don't let the looks of the squiggles that look like this: ><?\ a< scare you. For the most part, RSS is a simple copy-and-paste function. For a very basic guide to writing your own codes, find Tony Eldridge's little video tutorial at http://budurl.com/HTMLTutorial

Icon is a symbolic pattern or picture that represents something else. The **avatars** that appear when someone subscribes to your blog are examples of a photograph or artistic icon. Icons like the little orange one Google uses for their blog service are more like graphic designs or logos.

Keywords are the broad categories or the most essential words people use when they are searching for something specific on the Web. Knowing the keywords that best describe your store and your products can help you understand your own **branding** (see the entry on branding in this glossary).

Links are addresses to other places online. Sometimes they're just the raw **URL**s and sometimes they're key words with one of those URLs hiding behind them. When a reader clicks on a link, it is like pouring boiling water onto instant coffee. You get the fix you are after immediately. Links is also a catchall term for **incoming links, internal links,** and **back links**. It is important that you use links liberally for entities that you talk about in your blog. Blogger / Blogspot makes it easy to do that with a world-shaped **icon** at the top of the **posting window** for linking anything your heart desires.

New Media is a term we use for online media as opposed to the **old media** of print, TV, and radio.

Old Media are all the things we used to think of when we used the word "press" with TV and radio thrown into the mix.

Opt in is a term used to mean that an Internet user has given his or her permission to receive information in their e-mail boxes. If one has opted in, the message or post can't be considered spam. If tech sorts used real good, old-fashioned English instead of jargon, they'd just say people had "subscribed" to receive something delivered directly to them.

Podcast is the term used for little audio presentations you can install on your blog using **HTML** code and the **gadgets** that Blogger / Blogspot provides. Think of them as online radio for your visitors to listen to while they work at something else online.

Posting Window is the space on your blog where you type in or copy and paste the text for your posts or blog entries.

RSS Feed means Real Simple Syndication. Though it looks daunting, it is merely **HTML** code that makes your online life more efficient. Some important and free tools like Twitter and Google's online calendar let you install their features on your blogs, Web site, and **social networks** using HTML codes.

Search is something we do to find what we need on the Web. As an example, we search for other bloggers on general search engines like Yahoo or on engines provided by our **social networks**. We use **keywords** to find them so we can partner or cross promote with them.

Social Media / Social Networks are broad terms for Web sites where people go to commiserate with one another. They include MySpace, Facebook, Squidoo, eCademy, Plaxo, and many others. Retailers who use more than one of these venues should integrate them so they drive traffic, one to the other.

Tagline is a term often used instead of "credit." It is a mini biography or information piece (usually from twenty-five to 100 words) that includes **links** to your online entities like your blog, your Web site, and even your **social networks** like Facebook and LinkedIn.

Trailer is used in blogging much as it is used in the movie industry. Trailers are visual sales tools, often a combination of video, voiceover, music, and rolling or still print messages. When done professionally, they can be powerful (but nonessential) entities on your blog. When produced by people without marketing and design expertise the results can be downright silly.

URL refers to any Web address. Some editors are on a campaign to ditch the term altogether and call them simply . . . you know . . . "Web addresses." Even the initials are unwieldy—so much so people have come to pronounce them "Earl."

Widgets are easy linked logos from third-party providers that make it easier to travel from place to place on the Web, to subscribe to blogs and other entities, and to let your visitors let their readers know about your blog. One you see frequently is the green retweet widget from Tweetmeme.com that lets your visitors pass the information on your blog to their Twitter followers.

**APPENDIX TWO: STUDY FOR BETTER WRITING—
FRUGALLY**

Blogging almost certainly entails writing, unless you
choose to use videos and **podcasts** exclusively,
certainly a model for some to consider. That way a
blogger would only need to write headlines for the blog
and short introductions the podcast or video he or she
posts.

For those who enjoy writing or are interested in using
blogging as an adventure in improving your writing,
here are some ways to do that:

- Some words are magic. If you know them, your
  advertising, tweets, blog, and Web site will be
  more effective. Although Dr. Frank Luntz is a
  political animal, he makes an effort (not quite
  successfully) to be politically evenhanded in his
  *Words That Work: It's Not What You Say, It's
  What People Hear* (Hyperion). Regardless of
  your politics (or his), Luntz is the Republican
  word maestro who turned the term *estate tax*
  into *death tax*. It is for the words that motivate
  people positively, however, that you want to
  read his book: budurl.com/wordsthatwork.
- My *The Frugal Editor: Put Your Best Book
  Forward to Avoid Humiliation and Ensure
  Success* is a book that will help you edit your
  copy be it a blog or one of those freebie
  booklets we talked about. It will also help you
  format those booklets or whitepapers for a
  professional look. It won USA Book News Best

Publishing Book, Reader Views Literary First Place Award and the promotion campaign for it won the New Generation First Place Award for marketing. Published by Red Engine Press, find it at budurl.com/TheFrugalEditor.

- June Casagrande's two books are lots more fun than any grammar thing you ever tackled in school. *Grammar Snobs Are Great Big Meanies* (Penguin) is at budurl.com/grammarsnobs and her *Mortal Syntax* (Ten Speed Press) is at budurl.com/mortalsyntax. Both will help you do a little brushing up in preparation for you blogging experience.
- My *Great Little Last-Minute Editing Tips for Writers: The Ultimate Frugal Booklet for Avoiding Word Trippers and Crafting Gatekeeper-Perfect Copy* is a handy booklet that can be tucked into your briefcase. It will remind you of the some of the tricky homonyms you may have forgotten. Published by HowToDoItFrugally Publishing, it is only $6.95 new. Find it at budurl.com/WordTrippersPB.

  Hint: When you see capital letters in Web addresses, be sure to use them or you may not arrive at your intended destination.

- Subscribe to and get used to looking up style choices at Chicago Manual of Style at: www.chicagomanualofstyle.org.

Blogs are absolutely free, but you must be a more careful about using them as sources rather than other books which have been run through the publishing industry's filter for expertise. My Frugal, Smart and

Tuned-In Editor blog is at thefrugaleditor.blogspot.com and you'll find Grammar Girl Mignon Fogarty's blog at: grammar.quickanddirtytips.com. She covers basic grammar and some advanced stuff, too.

Don't overlook the buyer education programs at tradeshows. Administrators go to great expense to present the industry's best.

Here's a little more about saving. Use the new and used feature on online bookstores to get books inexpensively. If you purchase books new and spend over $25, shipping is usually free. In most states, there is no sales tax. Further, books and magazines that help you with your business are tax deductible, but you knew that.

At tradeshows, register early rather than pay more for seminars at the door.

APPENDIX THREE: SAMPLE BLOG ENTRY

This sample of a casual blog post shows you how to integrate your blog with your tweets and, by extension, how you can adapt it to blog about your other online or in-store efforts.

Cozy Cottage Tweets Specials

Get out your calendar and circle every Monday. That's the day we'll be Tweeting specials on merchandise that our customers will love. Once you know about them—anything from free booklets to in-store gifts-with-purchase—they're yours for the asking. Find us on line at www.CozyCottage.com, call us with your order at (800)790-XXXX, or come into one of our six locations (We've listed them all in the left column of this blog).

The thing is, you have to ask. The other thing is, the only place we'll be talking about them is on Twitter. Yes, we want you to Tweet with us because Twitter is fun. And because we want to get information to you fast. Information on new products, new bargains, fun events, and—generally—what's happening at our cottage.

You never know what the special might be. It might be free shipping to keep you from driving across town in the rain or to encourage folks in New York to try our down-home style. It might be a discount on something you rarely see on sale, like our brand name crystal. It might be a drawing for a gift basket filled with gift certificates from businesses around our town or around the nation.

Or it might be a mouth-blown glass bluebird from Terra Studios. We all know how bluebirds love to Tweet.

Tweet with us at www.Twitter.com/cozycottage
We blog at www.cozycottage.blogspot.com.

Entries in your blog might include different angles on the same subject framed as teasers. As an example, leading up to this invitation, you might have posted a blog on new stationery with a bluebird design and asked people to subscribe to your blog so they wouldn't miss why you are especially excited about this particular gift item.

You can also post teaser-blogs. Blogs based on these two ideas would get posted before events.

"Watch this blog for news of our new Fan page on Facebook."

Or

"Subscribe to this blog so you don't miss the news about our big USC vs. Stanford party in September.

APPENDIX FOUR: SAMPLE MEDIA RELEASE

Use 8 1/2 x 11 inch plain whitepaper of good quality when you send a media release by post. It should be no more than one page. Use "Media Release: (subject of release here)" in the subject line when you e-mail a release. Find complete detailed instructions on media relations, media kits, and formatting releases in *The Frugal Book Promoter: How To Do What Your Publisher Won't* (www.budurl.com/FrugalBkPromo).

Notice the title of the release. In addition to other media people, it is meant to attract the attention of business page editors looking for a local business person expert in the wiles and wonders of blogging. To appeal to online media, choose a different title, one that might attract the Web site owners and bloggers you will send it to. You would, of course, also tweak the release itself to give it more appeal for denizens of the Web.

M E D I A   R E L E A S E

Contact: Maggie Hollister
Phone: 818-790-XXXX
Fax: 818-790-XXXX
E-mail: Hollister@CozyCottage.com

For Immediate Release

Local Retailer Blogs for Benefit of Customers

Falls Church, VA—Get out your calendar and circle

every Monday. That's the day Jean King, our erstwhile staff member of 25 years, will be blogging specials that our Falls Church customers will love. Once you know about one of our specials, it's yours for the asking. Find us on line at www.CozyCottage.com, call us with your order at (818)790-XXXX, or come into one of our six locations.

The thing is, you have to ask. And the only place we'll be talking about these specials is on our Fine Linen Web Stationery blog. Yes, we want shoppers in Falls Church to follow us because blogging is fun, for us and fun for customers who can join in discussions with comments, win our contests, and benefit from blog-only bargains.

You never know what the special might be. It might be free shipping to keep you from driving cross town in the rain or to encourage folks in New York to try our down-home style. It might be a discount on something you rarely see on sale, like our brand name crystal. It might be a drawing for a gift basket filled with gift certificates from businesses around our town or around the Great Web World.

Find us blogging at
www.finelinenstationery.blogspot.com.
Tweet with us at www.Twitter.com/cozycottage
Come friend us at
www.Facebook.com/cozycottage.

Support materials are available on request.

Hint: Note the pound signs at the end of

the media release. They are one of many signs of a professional publicist. You'll want to use active links when you send your release by e-mail. If you're sending it by post, remove the underlines in those same Web addresses.

"Careers that are not fed soon die as readily as any living organism given no sustenance."

Index

Advertise in Future *Survive and Thrive* Books. Contact Carolyn at HoJoNews@aol.com

Advertise in Future *Survive and Thrive* Books. Contact Carolyn at HoJoNews@aol.com

Advertise in Future *Survive and Thrive* Books. Contact Carolyn at HoJoNews@aol.com

Advertise in Future *Survive and Thrive* Books. Contact Carolyn at HoJoNews@aol.com

About the Author

Carolyn Howard-Johnson puts nearly three decades of retail experience plus oodles more in the fields of journalism, public relations, publishing, and marketing into her *Survive and Thrive* series of books. She consults in the three Ps, publishing, promotion, and publicity, and is the author of the multi award-winning  HowToDoItFrugally series of books for writers and several award-winning books of fiction and poetry.

Howard-Johnson founded and operated stores ranging from home décor to gifts to antiques and other collectibles. She also owned and operated the souvenir shop at the world renowned Santa Anita Race Track. She served on the boards of directors of periodicals like *Gift Beat*, of the malls where her stores were located, and on the boards of cooperative catalogs her stores utilized. She also served on the California Gift Show board of directors. She has written for assorted industry periodicals including *Home Décor Buyer* and *LA Mart*. She puts this world of experience in retailing to work for you with this series of *Survive and Thrive* books and in private consultations.

Howard-Johnson was named Woman of the Year in Arts and Entertainment by members of the California Legislature. American Business Women's Association Impact Council also named her Woman of the Year and *Pasadena Weekly* honored her for literary activism. Her Web site is HowToDoItFrugally.com. She blogs at www.frugalretailing.blogspot.com.